ISBN:9973-700-86-4

Aïcha Ben Abed Ben Khader

THE
BARDO MUSEUM

a guided tour

Translated by
Gertie and Joël Bagage

cérès
EDITIONS

TUNISIA,
A CROSSROADS
IN HISTORY

Tunisia is a small country with an immense historical past covering several millenias.

Situated on the Mediterranean to the extreme North of the African continent and within easy reach of Europe, Tunisia is one of the jewels of these shores.

The first traces of man found here go back some two million years with, among other evidence, the prehistoric site near Chott El Jerid in Southern Tunisia.

Since that time several prehistoric civilisations have thrived on Tunisian soil, among them the prestigious Capsian civilisation which developed in the region of Gafsa - the ancient *Capsa* - , between the 7th and 5th millenia.

Tunisia entered history with the coming of the Phoenicians. From the 11th century BC onwards they set up trading posts along these hospitable shores. An ancient legend tells the story of the Queen of Tyr, Elyssa, who fled her native country to found a new city, Quart Hadasht, Carthage. Whatever the truth may be, the new city thrived tremendously and soon became one of the great metropolises of the Mediterranean. Carthage set about establishing a vast empire not only in Africa, but also in Sicily, Sardinia, Spain, etc. The great Greek historian Thucydides says that the Carthaginian fleet was the strongest in the world.

Rome waged three bloody wars against Carthage during the 2nd and 3rd centuries B.C. before bringing the great city to heel. Once again a legend tells us that Carthage, gone up in flames and smothered under a mountain of salt, became a city cursed by the gods of Rome.

Only with Caesar and later with Augustus did Rome and Carthage eventually become totally reconciled. The Romanisation of Carthage and her territories was a great asset for the Roman Empire, Carthage becoming, as it were, a platform for the development and prosperity of the Empire in *Africa*. Once again Carthage became a great metropolis and the capital city of a province known as «the granary of Rome».

The policy of Rome during the 2nd and 3rd centuries was to promote the economy of the region. The result was that the development and cultural influence of Africa reached their highest point at that period.

Not only do literary records of the time bear witness to this golden age but so does the wealth and variety of the many archaeological vestiges found throughout Tunisia which speak of the splendour of her Roman past.

In the 3rd century Christianity made its first timid appearance which culminated in a triumphant period between the 4th and the 7th centuries. Some of the great names of the early Christian Church come from Tunisia: *Tertullian*, Saint *Augustine*, Saint *Cyprian*.

Though conquered by the Vandals in the 5th century, «Africa Romana» (Roman Africa) remained an essential entity in the Mediterranean world.

But there could be no rest for the Byzantine Empire, the direct descendant of the Roman Empire, until it had taken Carthage back from Vandal hands.

Yet the country they won back had been weakened and ravaged by too many wars and passions, so that the Muslim armies of the mid-7th century easily overran a country too weary to retaliate. In the year 670 the Muslims founded their own capital city, Kairouan, situated at some distance from the seaboard, thus turning their backs on Carthage for ever.

Under the reigns of the *Aghabide* and *Fatimide* dynasties, Kairouan was to become the great capital city of Muslim Maghreb. Boosted by a prosperous economy it played an important role in the intellectual life of the Muslim World. In fact Kairouan was to become a major centre of Islamic civilisation where the great theologians and men of letters and science of the time gathered to seek spiritual and intellectual renewal. The great Mosque of Kairouan still stands today as a living example of the splendour of Islamic architecture.

Among other towns founded after Kairouan and marked out for great destinies was Mahdia, established by the same Fatimide princes who were to be the founders of Cairo.

The decision of the Hafside dynasty in the 13th century, to make Tunis - less than 20 kms from ancient Carthage - their capital city, marked the reconciliation of the *Ifriqyans* with the Mediterranean. This was the signal for the start of a new cycle of conquests and invasions coming from the direction of the sea. The first in line were the Spaniards, then came the Turks, followed in turn by the French who colonised Tunisia in 1881.

In 1956 Tunisia conquered her place among independant nations and with a clear vision of her historical past defined herself as Arabic, African and Mediterranean.

THE BARDO MUSEUM

The National Bardo Museum, already one hundred years old, keeps collections of historical and archeological objects relating to the history of Tunisia from prehistory to the end of the 19 th century and the early 20 th century. The thousands of objects that constitute the Museum collections are distributed among about fifty rooms and galleries of a bey's superb palace that was built largely in mid - 19 th century. The monument is interesting because of the hispano-Moresque style of its architecture, the «décor» of its ceilings with painted wood and sculpted plaster and of its walls covered by ornamented ceramics. The collections exhibited at the Bardo Museum are exclusively relating to the diverse civilizations that Tunisia has known. These collections, some of which are famous throughout the world, reflect well the diversity and the wealth of the Tunisian patrimony.

PREHISTORIC ANTIQUITIES

A visit of the Bardo Museum starts with collections from the prehistory and early history of Tunisia.

To your right in the hall, collections of flint blades, bones, costume ornaments and engraved stones from the Acheulean, Mousterian, Ibero-Moorish, Capsian and Neolithic eras. These collections give ample evidence of the presence of man on Tunisian soil from the earliest times.

The monument called «Hermaion of El Guettar» is of exceptional interest. Found at the foot of a spring in Southern Tunisia, it is made of a heaped pile of pebbles, balls of flint and bones. This monument is considered today as being one of the oldest ritual structures ever made by man.

Before coming to the Punic department you will see a display of objects belonging to early Tunisian history in the megalithic monuments and the *haouanet*. From here on you will find yourself in the world of Carthage with collections telling the story of six centuries of an illustrious past.

Staircase leading to first storey of the Museum. Series of pavements displayed on the walls, many of which are mosaics from funeral monuments of the Christian era : in the rear, a statue of Apollo from Carthage.

«Hermaion» of El Guettar (near Gafsa) from the Mousterian age. This cone-shaped pile, about 0.75m in height and 1.50m in diameter is made up of over 4,000 pieces of flint, stone and limestone pellets. This votive

monument, probably dedicated to the «spirit» of a spring, is thought to be one of the first expressions of man's spiritual quest.

PUNICO-LIBYC COLLECTION

Dominating the room is an effigy of the god *Baal-Hammon*, head of the Carthaginian Pantheon. This is in fact a small statue in terra-cotta from the first century A.D. found in a rural sanctuary at Thinissut, near Bir Bou Rekba (cf map) and it proves the continuing worship of the Punic god long after the destruction of Carthage in 146 B.C. A group of three divinities in the same room shows *Pluto*, *Demeter* wearing the *polos* and *Kore* carrying a piglet. These large terra-cotta statues come as a surprise, probably made as they were from Greek moulds of the 4th century B.C. Also here is the very famous 4th century B.C. Priest and Child stele with an engraving in profile of a priest carrying a child on his left arm in readiness for sacrifice.

A collection of objects for ritual purposes is displayed in the following room : perfume-braziers, symbols, bells. There are also some fine examples of Carthaginian razors and different objects in pottery and other materials imported from the major Mediterranean cities trading with Carthage.

The visitor will now come to the very famous collection of grimacing masks; these masks vary in size and are made in «pâte de verre» or pottery and were used to frighten away evil spirits. The refined elegance of the Carthaginian lady is illustrated in the collection of objects for personal adornment such as ivory fibulae, pearl necklaces and cosmetic boxes.

Baal-Hammon. Temple of Thinissut (Cape Bon), 1st century A.D. A terra-cotta statuette representing the principal god of the Carthaginians, wearing a crown of feathers and seated on a throne. The arm-rests of the throne represent sphinxes.

Above : Terra-cotta mask of grimacing man, 7th century B.C. In the Punic era masks of this type were placed in tombs to ward off evil spirits.

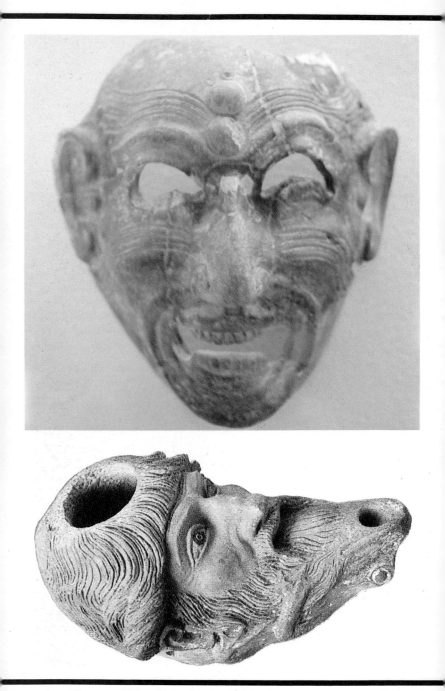

Below : Terra-cotta lamp. Kerkouane (Cape Bon), 3rd century B.C. Top part in shape of a bearded man's head, lower part in shape of a frog.

Left : Stele from the Ghorfa plain (near Dougga), 3rd century A.D. One of a series, this stele is of flattened obelisk shape.
Above, a spirit of fertility with kantharos (drinking cup) and bunch of grapes. Also two gods. In the centre, the facade of a temple with the dedicating priest.

Right : Stela of the Tophet of Carthage, 3rd century B.C. A priest carrying a child about to be offered in sacrifice.

The older Punic artistic tradition survived the destruction of Carthage well into the Roman period, as can be seen here from the *Punic* and neo-Punic stelae, richly carved and bearing inscriptions varying in content.

The Punic tomb displayed in a smaller adjoining room is well worth seeing: the skeleton, the wall paintings, the arrangement of the funeral objects on display are a reconstruction from a tomb found at Cap Bon.

After the Punic section the visitor will see some documents relating to the *Libyc* civilisation from which Tunisia takes its roots: two bas-reliefs showing gods of the Libyc Pantheon found in the heart of *Numidia*, in the North-West of Tunisia. Also displayed are some stelae, mostly funeral monuments, with bilingual inscriptions in Libyc and Punic or Libyc and Latin.

Of special note is the bilingual inscription of Dougga commemorating the dedication of a temple to *Masinissa* in 126 B.C. together with a stela representing eight godheads with a goddess in the centre.

On the first floor the room displaying **Punic jewelry** opens on to the **Virgil room**. Some of the jewels displayed here are from the 7th century B.C. Most of them come from Carthage but there are also pieces from Utica and Kerkouane. There are some fine sets of matching necklaces and earrings, rings, pendant seals, amulet cases and *prophylactic* strips.

This jewelry is mostly in solid gold. The typical Carthaginian technique incorporating a bronze core with an outer covering of gold is also used. Oriental and Greek iconography are the sources of inspiration for the decorative motifs.

Below : Punic gold coins. Profile of a woman on the obverse ; a horse on the reverse (shown here).

ROMAN AND PALEO-CHRISTIAN DEPARTMENT

In spite of the wealth and diversity of the prehistoric, Punic and Islamic collections, the Bardo Museum remains famous above all for its Roman and *Paleo-Christian* collections, with particular emphasis on its mosaics.

On leaving the Libyc section the visitor will see some of the renowed stelae of Ghorfa, from the 3rd century A.D. They give a very clear picture of the *syncretism* which had taken place at that period between the Roman and Libyco-Punic religion.

The interest of these stelae lies less in their workmanship - in fact still rather clumsy - than in the fact that they illustrate the sharp change from African beliefs to the religion of the Romans, with a marked preference for *Saturn* who was given pride of place in the Romano-African *Pantheon*.

On the way towards the stela corridor, two very fine 2nd century marble sarcophagi are displayed. One bears a representation of the nine Muses, the other the four seasons pictured as children gathered around a dead young man.

In the same corridor there are two famous Roman artefacts. One is the funeral effigy of a Romano-African citizen represented as *Hercules* being initiated into the cult of Ceres. This 3rd century statue was at Borj El Amri. The other work, also from the 3rd century was found near Siliana. Known as the Boglio stele it belongs to a series of stelae dedicated to Saturn.

Roman Carthage Room, the former patio of the Palace. On the floor, mosaics from Oudna ; in the centre altar to the *Gens Augusta* ; carvings mostly from Carthage in surrounding space.

From this corridor the visitor goes on to the **Thuburbo Majus room** which bears the name of the site where the vast collection of objects here on display was found. Particularly interesting is the small bas-relief representing *Maenads* from the 1st century A.D. in the pure Hellenistic tradition. Different monuments on this site yielded the inscriptions, statues, marble wall panelling and geometrical and floral mosaics displayed here.

The visitor must now retrace his steps to reach the Paleo-Christian department with its great collections of tomb mosaics and church pavements. Within this collection some mosaics are outstanding, in particular the one bearing the inscription *Ecclesia Mater* and

known by that name. The subject matter of this mosaic is especially interesting. It represents a section of a church with *apse*, *naves*, *altar*, roof and even the mosaic paving. It is a 4th century work and was found at Tabarka.

Another tomb mosaic of great interest shows two people on different levels : On the top register, the man seated behind a desk is identified by some experts as being a notary public, while others see him as a banker. On the lower register an *orant* figure called «Victoria» is thought to be the notary's daughter because of the age difference. The mosaic represents seven crowns inside of which the names of seven martyrs are inscribed, among them Saint Stephen. This is obviously a precious

Tomb mosaic. Tabarka. 4th century A.D. Section of a church. Easily discernable are the entrance with its steps, the nave, the altar with lighted candles, even the mosaic paving representing doves.

document concerning the history of Christianity in Africa.

The paving of a church at Oued Remel shows the faithful building a monument, probably the church itself.

In the centre of the room is a fine limestone *baptismal* font found at Gightis.

The presence and impact of Christianity in Africa between the 4th and 7th centuries is also illustrated by the collection of tiles showing Biblical scenes.

The **Bulla Regia Room** houses a remarkable group from the Temple of Apollo, among them Apollo *Citharedes*, *Aesculapius* and Ceres.

The smaller adjoining room to the back displays a collection of portraits of Roman emperors.

The walls of the staircase leading from the ground-floor to the rooms and galleries on the first floor are hung with various types of tomb mosaics from Tabarka dating from the 4th to the 6th centuries. They either show the deceased as an orant or illustrate Christian symbols such as the *Christogram* with an *epitaph* giving the name of the deceased, his age and on occasion his occupation.

These mosaics supply us with precious insights into the origins, average age and activities of the African population. They are also a source of information on the styles of different workshops of the period.

On the first floor the visit begins with the **Carthage Gallery**. Of imposing proportions with its colonnade

Above right : Statue of the Emperor Hadrian as a hero (detail). Carthage, 2nd century.

Below : Sarcophagus of the Nine Muses (detail). Porto Farina, 3rd century. Subject frequently seen in late Antiquity, the idea being to praise the deceased, a man of culture and friend of the Muses (*mousikos anêr*).

Above : Mosaic from the *Laberii* House. Oudna, 3rd century. Bacchus-Dionysus offering the vine to Ikarios in the presence of the King of Attica.

Below : Mosaic from the *Laberii* House. Oudna, 3rd century. Very lively picture of the various activities on a rural estate: labours of the field and hunting.

and high ornamented ceiling, this gallery displays a fine collection of sculpture mainly from Carthage. There are numerous Roman gods and colossal portraits of an empress and of the Emperor Hadrian. A very important piece in the centre of the gallery is an altar dedicated to the *Gens Augusta* with carved bas-reliefs on all four sides. The first side shows Aeneas fleeing Troy with his father Anchises and his son Ascanius. The carving on the second side represents a personification of Rome wearing a helmet, seated on a stack of arms and holding a sword and a trophy. A cornucopia placed on an altar is facing the figure of Rome. On the third side a sacrificial scene is depicted probably with *Augustus* making libations with the aid of assistants. On the fourth side Apollo, protector of the Gens Augusta is portrayed seated on the cithara and tripod, the attributes of Apollo. It is generally accepted that this monument dates back to between the 1st century B.C. and the 1st century A.D.

The two famous 3rd century mosaic pavements laid out on the floor of the Carthage Gallery are from the so-called Laberii house at Oudhna, the ancient Uthina. The central feature in the first pavement, of meticulous workmanship depicts a mythological scene with Bacchus offering the vine to the peasant Ikarios in the presence of the King of *Attica*. Surrounding the scene is a decorative composition of a vine peopled with harvesting cupids.

The second mosaic in the patio shows various outdoor activities: ploughing, sowing, bringing home the livestock, olive-picking and diverse hunting scenes.

Displayed in the **Oudhna Room** - once the dining-room of the palace - are other mosaics, among them four small but splendid masterpieces. The motifs of superb precision and delicacy are mounted on terra-cotta and known as *emblemata* (inlaid work). Two of them show the remains of a meal. A large paving pictures Orpheus charming animals as he plays the lyre.

A large number of other scenes related either to mythology or hunting are displayed on the walls of the room.

The collections from the **maritime excavations of Mahdia** are to be found in the rooms adjoining the other side of the patio. The wealth of material here was discovered by sponge-divers at the beginning of this century and corresponds to the cargo of a ship which had left Greece for either Sicily or Italy and foundered off the coast of Tunisia. The excavation yielded a treasure of renowned *Hellenistic* bronze and marble pieces. The visitor will see the Agon and *Hermes* group, dwarf dancers, bronze statues of gods, beds, other pieces of furniture and some household utensils. Also on display are the equally famous marble statues of Aphrodite deeply scarred by their long immersion in the sea, various architectural components, enormous carved kraters and of course the wrecked ship itself.

The adjoining rooms house the collection of marine mosaics with sections of a huge mosaic from Carthage. The architectural design around its border

Oudhna mosaics, 1st century. These small pictures knows as emblemata are made from tiny tesserae. Two of them show the remains of a meal (*asarôtos oikos*) and belong to a style created in the Hellenistic era.

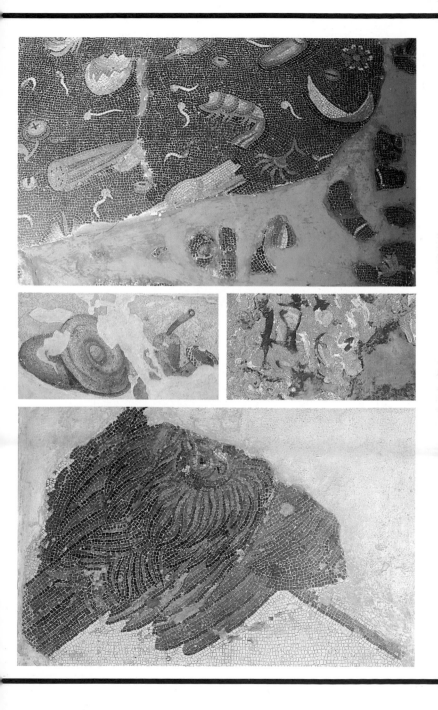

Maritime excavations of Madhia. Bronze statue of a young satyr preparing to spring forward. 2nd to 1st century B.C.

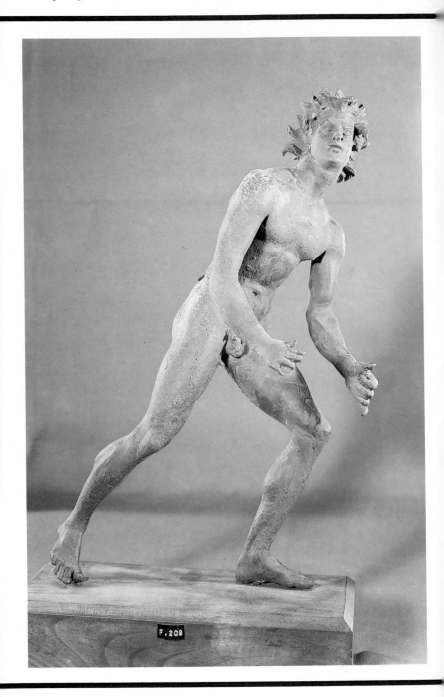

Maritime excavations of Madhia. Marble bust of Aphrodite damaged from lengthy stay in the sea. 2nd-1st century B.C.

encloses fantastic mythical sea-scenes showing grottoes and dolphins dominated by nereids riding sea creatures. Some other scenes with sea creatures show the fascination of Africans for maritime themes of decoration in the 3rd and 4th centuries.

The Mausoleum Room gives ample opportunity to assess the wealth and diversity of the African mosaicist's creativity. Displayed on the walls of the great room are pictures from Thuburbo Majus among them the very lovely carpet of the heads and shoulders of animals from the world of the amphitheatre. The crowning of Venus, dancers and fishermen with their boats among shoals of fish complete the picture. In the centre of the room the vast *mausoleum* of a carthaginian is displayed. Carved reliefs decorate all four sides of the monument.

The visitor must retrace his steps to the Carthage gallery and from there continue to the **Virgil Room**. This octagonal hall gave access to the Bey's private apartments. Above the hall the magnificent dome is decorated with carved plasterwork. The room takes its name from the very famous mosaic of the Latin poet displayed there. This 3rd century mosaic found at Sousse shows Virgil seated in meditation holding a papyrus inscribed with the eighth line of the *Aeneid*. To his right, Clio, the Muse of history, to his left Melpomene, the Muse of tragedy. The mosaic found in the house of a Roman citizen at Sousse is the oldest representation of the poet to have survived to our day.

Above : Carthage mosaic, Byrsa Hill, 4th century. A Nereid. Detail of a huge paving representing a fantastic seascape with sea monsters and Nereids.

Below : Virgil Room. A room in the Bey's private apartment with its remarkable stuccoed ceiling. Famous mosaic discovered at Sousse. (cf p. 38-39).

Above : Bir Chana mosaic (near Zaghouan). 3rd century. Medallions with signs of the zodiac and godheads of the days of the week.

Below : Carthage mosaic. 4th century. Banqueting scene (detail). Note that the guests are sitting on benches and not in a recumbent position as was then the custom.

The mosaic of Bir Chana (near Zaghouan) is displayed in the centre of the floor. The outer series of medallions shows the signs of the zodiac on a background imitating Chemtou marble, a material much prized at the time. The inner frieze represents the seven godheads of the week: Luna (Monday), Mars (Tuesday), Mercury (Wednesday), Jupiter (Thursday), Venus (Friday), Sol (Sunday). Dominating the centre is Saturn (Saturday).

On leaving the Virgil Room and after going through the patio again, the visitor will enter the long **Althiburos Room**, symmetric with its companion the Oudhna Room. This is where the palace concerts were given. The series of mosaics here belongs mainly to Althiburos and Carthage.

Laid on the floor is a 4th century mosaic representing a complete catalogue of Roman boats with each vessel given its correct title in Greek or Latin. The god of the Ocean and the god of the River are represented at either end of the picture.

Another famous Carthaginian mosaic of the same period represents a banqueting scene. It is opposite the doorway and shows guests seated on benches behind tables. They are receiving food and drink from the servants while musicians and dancers occupy the centre of the picture. This mosaic is a valuable source of information on the social life of the well-to-do Carthaginians of the 4th century.

Dougga Room. Painted ceiling of the old palace.

Oudna Room (ancient *Uthina*), the palace's former dining-room. On the rear wall, the *Laberii* House mosaic where Orpheus is seen charming animals.

In the same room another Carthaginian mosaic is known as «*Hunting the Crane*». It represents a hunting scene, a much sought-after pastime of the African aristocracy. Statues of Appolo and Diana inside a temple can be seen in the centre of the picture. The hunters standing in front of an altar are offering a crane in sacrifice to the gods. In the central motif hunting scenes are represented with masters and servants alike giving chase. Belonging to the height of the Christian period (5th to 7th centuries), this mosaic clearly demonstrates the survival of certain pagan practices.

From here, through the Carthage gallery, the visitor's steps will take him to the huge **Sousse Room**. In addition to a large collection of mosaics from Sousse, Carthage and Tabarka, the head and feet of a colossal statue of Jupiter from the Capitol of Thuburbo Majus are also on display.

Also to be seen are collections of Punic, Greek and Roman lamps, and ceramic ware known as «*sigillated* African pottery» from the famous ceramic workshops of El Aouja near Kairouan. The floor is largely covered by the superb 3rd century mosaic found in the house of Sorothus, a horse-breeder from Sousse. The central motif shows Neptune in triumph surrounded by his retinue of sea creatures.

The splendid «Lord Julius» mosaic is one of the great treasures of the Bardo Museum. The picture shows scenes in the life of Julius, a high personage of the time. The centre of the mosaic shows the great

Below : Sousse mosaic, 3rd century. Neptune in triumph. Detail from a huge pavement in the house of Sorothus, a horse-breeder.

Sousse mosaic, 3rd century. The poet Virgil is seen holding a *volumen* (papyrus roll) inscribed with the eighth line of the Aeneid.

To his right, Clio, the Muse of history, also holding a volumen; to his left, Melpomene, the Muse of tragedy, holding a mask.

Above: The «*Lord Julius*» mosaic, found in Carthage. Early 5th century. On three registers and surrounding the buildings of a rich villa, the various activities of a rural domain in late Antiquity are shown. Master, mistress and servants can be seen. The backgound setting shows the cycle of the seasons of the year.

Below: detail of the *Lord Julius* mosaic. The lady of the house is dressing, with the aid of a handmaid bearing a jewel box and presenting a necklace to her mistress.

40

arcaded, turretted and domed mansion of the Lord of the Manor. On the lowest register in the left-hand corner, Lord Julius is seen, seated in the shade of a tall tree, stretching out his hand to receive a message on a scroll brought to him by a tenant. On the same level his wife, dressing, is waited on by her servants. To the left of the mansion, the lord himself, on horseback is leaving for the hunt followed by a servant while to the right two helpers with hounds are opening the way for the hunt. On the top register the household goddess, protectress of the estate, is seated in the shade of a cypress grove. She is holding a fan in her right hand. On either side tenants are seen bringing her offerings of produce from the domain. The four corners represent the four seasons. Roses for spring, olives for winter, wheat for summer and grapes for autumn.

These symbols are a clear indication of the wealth and prosperity of the lord's estate.

Displayed on the other walls of the room are three big pavings from apses showing other large private domains from Tabarka. They are probably from the same period as the Carthage mosaic.

Two other mosaics displayed here illustrate the Africans' passion for the circus and chariot races. The first paving is from Carthage and shows a circus-race in the 3rd century. The second shows a race and its spectators at Gafsa in the 6th century.

Mosaic from the Cyclop's Thermae (detail), Dougga. Probably 4th century. It shows three giants, the Cyclops, busy working in the forge of Vulcan, the god of Hell. Neither the gigantic character of the bodies nor their dark colour are very common in African mosaics.

In the **Dougga Room** you will see two ancient models of the city. One of the Square of the Capitol and the other of the theatre. Displayed on the walls and floor are mosaics from La Chebba, Carthage and Thuburbo Majus. Of particular interest is the very fine 2nd century floor covering found at La Chebba. Neptune in triumph on his chariot is represented in the central motif. The four seasons are positioned in the four corners while the corresponding labours of the months are shown on the sides. The outstanding composition

Neptune in triumph. La Chebba (near Sfax), late 2nd Century. Central medallion showing the sea-god on his chariot. In the corners representation of the four seasons through their characteristic vegetation (wheat, olive, vine, reed). On the sides, the labours of the month.

and workmanship of this mosaic are certainly the work of a great artist.

There is another fine and remarkably realistic mosaic opposite the Neptune exhibit. It represents cyclops working Vulcan's forge in his cavern. This mosaic is from the 4th century and was found in the Cyclop's thermae at Dougga. The other picture showing cup-bearers serving guests is from the same site of Dougga.

Above : Men playing dice, detail of a mosaic from the El Jem *triclinium*, 3rd century.

Below : *xenia* (still-life) mosaic from El Jem, 3rd century. Detail showing a gazelle, a duck, a hare and fish.

The El Jem mosaics displayed in the **El Jem Room** take their name from the site where they were found. Medallions from two large pavings represent *xenia* motifs, (i.e. related to comestibles and hospitality): animals, fish, vegetables, fruit and flowers, sometimes in association with animals from the circus, musical instruments and Dionysian masks. These subjects were often found in a dining-room (*triclinium*) and reflected the wealth and prosperity of the host. The mosaics here belong to the 3rd century. From the same period another mosaic laid on the floor shows Bacchus riding his triumphal chariot drawn by tigers in the company of members of his *godly* retinue : Silenus, maenads, satyrs, and the god Pan. Completing the picture, a somptuous decoration of vine bursting forth from kraters situated in the four corners covers the background.

The **Ulysses Room** is on the other side of the corridor. It takes its name and fame from the Ulysses mosaic found at Dougga on display here. The great hero of the Odyssey is portrayed standing, bound to the mast of his ship and listening rapturously to the song of the Sirens who are shown standing on the right. Ulysses' companions have stopped their ears with wax - as we are told in Homer's epic poem - so as not to hear the bewitching melody.

Other mosaics are displayed in this room, among them the huge Utica mosaic (late 3rd to early 4th century). The head of Oceanus is shown at the top of the picture while Neptune and Amphitrite are seen on a chariot drawn by sea-horses. Beneath them two Nereids

Above: Ulysses' mosaic. Dougga, 4th century. Illustrates an episode of Homer's Odyssey with Ulysses bound to his mast and listening in rapture to the bewitching song of the Sirens. The sailors, seated on either side of the hero have stopped their ears with wax and are looking away so as not to fall under the spell.

Centre: detail of the same mosaic: The Sirens. One of them is playing the double-flute, another, the lyre.

Below: detail: a sea-crayfish.

Above : The child Dionysus in the company of old Silenus, a Maenad and a Satyr, chastises the Tyrrhenian Sea pirates who have attacked him, and turns them into dolphins.

Centre : detail of the Ulysses' mosaic: The hero bound to the mast of his vessel, a ship with two sails and one tier of oars.

Below : The pirates' punishment mosaic : Silenus seated in the boat.

are seated on two sea-tigers. The central section of the paving is dominated by three boats carrying three richly-bejewelled female figures surrounded by cupids. Putti are seen above the boats playfully riding birds. The lowest part of the mosaic is peopled with centaurs and sea-creatures ridden by handsome Nereids.

In the same room another 4th century mosaic found at Carthage illustrates the crowning of Venus. The central motif shows Venus seated on a throne, the canopy of which is richly decorated with precious gems. The semi-nude goddess adorned with her jewels is placing a crown on her head. She is escorted on either side of her throne by musicians and dancing dwarves standing in boats sailing rich waters abounding in fish.

A fountain from Thuburbo Majus decorated with the head of Oceanus is displayed at one end of the room. The interior surfaces of the fountain are decorated with figures of Nereids and sea-monsters. This is a good example of the shape and ornamentation of this type of fountain found in the peristyle of the Africano-Roman house and situated in front of the largest room or *œcus*.

Above this architecural element there is a very lovely mosaic from El Jem. In the centre, a scene where Marsyas, the satyr, competes with Appolo in a musical contest, while Minerva is seen as the judge.

The corners are decorated with busts representing the four seasons and the sides with *kraters* brimming

The Crowning of Venus, 4th century (detail). The goddess seated on a canopied throne places a crown on her own head.

Above : Peacock spreading its tail.
Bir Chana (near Zaghouan), 3rd
century.

Below : Venus being crowned by
two female centaurs. Ell s (near
Mactar). Late 4th, early 5th century.

with the produce of each season. This mosaic is from the 3rd century, a period when mosaic production at El Jem and its region was at its apogee.

In **Room XXVIII** the 4th century paving of an apse, called «*Hunting the Wild Boar*» is displayed. This is one of the many illustrations on the subject of the hunt, an activity highly prized by the rich Africans of the 3rd, 4th and 5th centuries. The mosaic illustrates the three different stages of the boar hunt. The badly damaged lower part shows the sportsmen leaving for the hunt. Above them a servant is seen letting the hounds loose. They are rushing towards the boar which in turn is rushing forward into the net that has been stretched out to entangle it. On the top register the servants are seen carrying the dead boar home.

In the same room a rather unusual representation of Venus is displayed. The mosaic comes from Elles and shows the goddess being crowned by two female centaurs.

A third picture here depicts one of the favourite themes in 4th century Africa: triumphant horses. On the lower level four horses are seen grazing plants symbolizing the four seasons. These plants grow out of four valuable cylindrical vessels studded with gems. Above them a pea-cock, its tail spread, symbolizes eternity and renewal.

Indeed in an Africa with such a passion for games, chariot-races in the circus took pride of place.

Above : Bacchus in triumph. El Jem, 3rd century (detail). The god is seen standing in his chariot, drawn by two female tigers and driven by Pan.

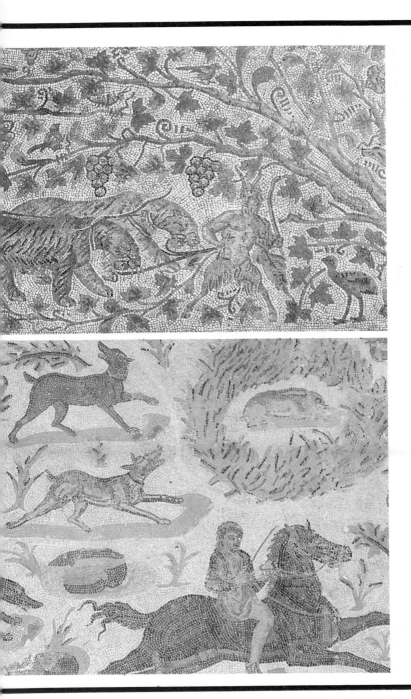

Below : El Jem mosaic, 3rd century. The various stages of a hunt. A hare chased by hounds is hiding in a bush.

Charioteers and victorious horses were, in the same way as today's *show-business stars*, the great heroes of the African city.

Leaving room XXVIII on the way to the second floor one can see a fine mosaic picturing the marriage of Bacchus and Ariane with a Dyonisian retinue celebrating the event. The mosaic is from a 4th century house in Thuburbo Majus.

In the show-cases on the galleries surrounding the Carthage patio on the second floor a wealth of objects found in necropolises of the 1st to the 3rd centuries are on display. They consist in phials, glasses, bowls, vessels and dishes which had been placed in the tombs of the deceased. There are funeral urns and a rich collection of bronze objects: masks, which served as sconces on furniture, statuettes of Venus, Victory, Mercury, Cupid, etc. The show-case on the left of the doorway contains a surgeon's kit with lancets and scalpels, forceps and trephines.

Another part of the gallery displays collections of terra-cotta statuettes ususally found in the temple, the tomb or the lararium. These grotesques and representations of protective gods such as Venus or Mercury, give us an accurate account of the religious beliefs of the time, unlike the monumental statuary which reflects the official ideology of the Empire.

In **Room XXX** more pavings give further proof of the enormous wealth of the mosaic collections of the Bardo Museum.

Above : A case of surgical instruments: scalpels, lancet, forceps, etc.
Centre : Roman lamps, 1st-2nd century

I. 2490

Below left : African sigillated ceramics with applique decorations.
Below right : anthropomorphic vase in the shape of old men's heads in superposition.

Theseus and the Minotaur. Thuburbo Majus, 4th century. This mosaic covered the floor of a thermae *frigidarium*. The hero is cutting off the monster's head among the debris of the labyrinth. The ground is strewn with remains of the Minotaur's victims.

From Thuburbo Majus another 4th century mosaic depicts Theseus slaying the Minotaur. The meandering loops of the Maze cover the ground while a fantasy rendering of the walls and gates of the city serves as a border to the whole.

A mosaic from El Jem shows another very popular theme in Africa in the person of a haloed Bacchus holding a *thyrsus* in one hand and a gecko in the other. A number of animals associated with the amphitheatre are in the company of the god. These animals and the games were very well-known to the Africans as most African cities had amphitheatres.

A 4th century mosaic displayed here, found at Thelepte (Fériana) represents a further view of the same subject. The central part of the picture shows a surprisingly realistic representation of a bloody combat between a bestiarius and a lion. A row of spectators is seated above them.

Another very interesting 2nd century paving shown here comes from Thuburbo Majus. Vegetation is omnipresent. In the centre of a medallion a poet is seen meditating over a *volumen* (papyrus roll). He is seated on a column shaft in front of an altar bearing two theatre masks. This is one of the many African mosaics in praise of intellectual and artistic pursuits.

Room XXXI displays an abundance of mosaics illustrating a variety of themes. From Thuburbo Majus in the 3rd century comes a Diana the Huntress riding a deer in the presence of two figures, one of whom is a gladiator. She is surrounded by a large number of animals of the amphitheatre.

A lovely threshold piece from Utica (3rd century) shows Venus seated on a rock and raising her hands in admonition towards the three cupids playing with her veil.

The last of the rooms on the second floor is the **Acholla Room**. The collections here are a clear indication of the wealth and creative ability of the city of Acholla, strongly influenced by what is known as the Byzacene School that developed around El Jem and Sousse. The mosaics were found in thermae or private houses. The wall opposite the doorway is covered in part with a large fragment from the *frigidarium* (cold room) of the so-called Trajan thermae.

A reproduction of a groin vault is part of the decoration of this mosaic. In the form of strips, it is an ornamentation with centaurs and wild animals shown in combat. Elsewhere small figures spring forth from a curvilinear decoration treated as foliage, while variations on the theme of the couple Satyr and Maenad are also treated.

Also from this frigidarium another mosaic representing vaulting, this time a barrel vault, with a very fine central medallion showing Dionysus in triumph. His chariot is drawn by two centaurs, and the two seasons, spring and winter, are portrayed on either

Above: Threshold mosaic from Utica, 3rd Century (detail). Venus seated on a rock.

Below : Diana the Huntress riding a deer surrounded by a number of animals from the amphitheatre.

side. Fragments of a second very similar mosaic were hung as a pair with the Dionysus scene. This group of pavings from the Trajan thermae belongs to the grand Hellenistic tradition bearing similarities in subject, composition and style.

Also from Acholla are two panels, one of which illustrates a *xenia* with baskets of fruit on a fine chequered arrangement of laurel leaves. The other one is decorated with busts of the four seasons on an identical background.

There are two T-shaped mosaics here (the central or T-shaped part of a dining-room mosaic was designed

Detail of the paving of the *frigidarium* in the Acholla thermae 2nd century. It represents the planning arrangement of a groin vault.

to be seen, while the U-shaped section was hidden by benches.) Again one of the themes is a *xenia* with baskets of fruit, some fowls and also four-legged animals. The other one relates the Labours of Hercules. A fountain decorated with a multitude of species of fish is also displayed here.

This room concludes the section of the Museum devoted to the Africano-Roman collections which, the visitor will no doubt have realized, are hard to equal in either quality or diversity.

A four-season mosaic. Acholla, 3rd Century. Busts of the four seasons on a chequered arrangement of laurel leaves.

The Circus mosaic, Carthage, 3rd century. Four quadrigae are shown racing on a track separated by a wall, the *spina*.

One of them is running counter to the direction of the other three. Note the representation of the circus wall with its two-storied facade.

Entrance to the Islamic department.

ISLAMIC DEPARTMENT

To get to the Islamic department, walk back through Rooms XXXI and XXX as far as the big second-floor gallery. Take the main staircase, from the corridor marked F which will bring you to the Carthage gallery. From here turn to your right and the Islamic department is straight on.

Two seats offered to the Bey of Tunis by Napoleon III can be seen in the hall. To the left a corridor gives access on both sides to rooms containing various artefacts. In one of these rooms to the right there are pieces in inlaid work, either imported to or copied in Tunisia. These collections are from the 18th and 19th centuries. Also on show are mirrors, chests, inlaid wooden clogs - mostly with mother-of-pearl - in geometrical or floral designs.

In a show-case to the right of the doorway a collection of musical instruments is exhibited : tambourines, *rhab* (a type of violin imported from Andalusia), zithers, a lute, etc..

In a smaller room is displayed a collection of weapons from the Middle-East and North Africa: sabres, swords, ornamented daggers, in some cases bearing inscriptions. A large show-case displays fire arms including rifles and pistols with inlaid decoration. In the room to the left there is a rich collection of household objects in copper: trays, cauldrons, vases, ewers, lamps, a *daghar* (brazier), etc.

The **Traditional Costume and Jewelry Room** is at the end of the corridor. Collections offer many objects in embossed silver: sprinklers, utensils, chests, jewelry from Tunis, from the interior of the country or from other regions of North Africa. Some items of dress for special occasions and specific to the city of Tunis are also displayed here.

Other aspects of traditional folk arts and traditions can be seen on the floor above by taking the stairs to the right. Show-cases display items in moulded ceramics from the region of Sejnane. The walls are hung with decorative ceramic panels of Andalusian, Moroccan, Turkish or Middle-Eastern origins.

By retracing his steps, the visitor will come to the jewel display room near the new hallway. To the left there is a lovely little open patio with a fine marble fountain in the centre. A series of long rooms gives onto the patio.

The room to the right displays a series of engravings from the 16th century, some of which show the storming of Tunis by Charles V of Spain.

The room opposite, in fact the main room of the palace, is of particular interest on account of its characteristic outlay. It contains a display of pieces of furniture and other objects from the late 19th century. The four-poster bed to the right is probably Venetian. The recess in the centre is furnished with couches and a whatnot. A screen, a cot and an armchair from the family of the Bey are shown to the left.

Above : Ceramic panel showing two fighting lions, made in El Kallaline, Tunis 19th century.

Below : *Daghar* or brazier, probably of oriental origin.

Pages from the Blue Koran, a famous manuscript from the Great Mosque of Kairouan, 11th century. The suras are written in letters of gold on sheets of blue parchment.

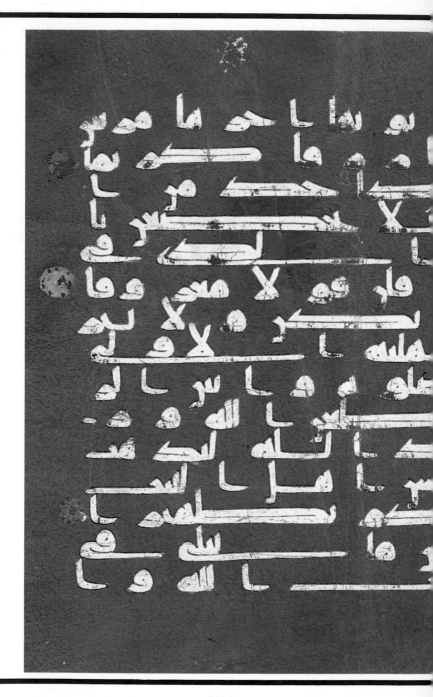

و همـا
فا اکحـک یا لهـ
لسا الـ لسـ
لسا ا العـ
لعو ل قـ
فله و مـ
و همـ ر
و حـ و سـ
و ا قمـ
کـو مـ
سـو ل نما لـ
کسـ ا لـ
و لـ طلهـ
و اکـ
لهو کـ ر ا

Above : Three-panelled screen in turned wood.

Below : Bas relief of the Fatimide era, Madhia, 10th-11th century representing a prince wearing a crown and listening to a woman playing the flute.

The third room contains a display of objects pertaining to Judaism, among them scrolls of the Torah.

On leaving the patio, take a few steps downwards to the left and once again to the left a few steps upwards to reach the room displaying collections related to Islam in the Middle-Ages. A wealth of material here covers many collections. Among them a series of manuscripts, e.g. pages from the famous 10th century Blue Koran of Kairouan written in Kufic style and pages from the Koran bequeathed to the Kairouan Mosque in 1020 and which had belonged to Fatma Al Hadhna, the nurse of Emir Zirid Mu'izz Ibn Badis.

Several other pages from the Kairouan Koran illustrate the calligraphy used in Maghreb in the 10th and 11th centuries.

Housed here is a collection of *tiraz*, fabrics bearing Koranic inscriptions or inscriptions in praise of the Prince, showing a steady progression in the elaborate character of the calligraphy. These materials from the Fatimide period were acquired in Egypt by the great Tunisian scholar Hassen Hosni Abdelwahab. There is also a *Fatimide bas-relief from Mahdia* (10th or 11th century) showing a musician playing the flute and a prince wearing a crown.

In the central show-cases the 11th century *Treasure of Tarabia* (near Kef) is on display, with gold necklaces, bracelets and earrings. In these show-cases, objects in bone, ivory and glass of Egyptian origin can also be seen.

Ceramic dish decorated with an antelope. Kairouan, 10th century.

Astrolabes, sun-dials and copper compasses from the 14th to the 19th centuries are here on display.

There is also a fine collection of gold and silver coins from various parts of Maghreb and the Middle-East.

Two big show-cases contain collections of Muslim ceramics from the Abasside period onwards. The various Ifriquian styles since the Aghabide period are of special interest.

On leaving the Islamic department you will reach a *driba* (entrance hall) furnished with sofas and where a model of the Ribat of Sousse is exhibited.

Glass decanter. Sabra, 10th century.

Here the visit of the Bardo Museum comes to an end. The visitor has been offered an accurate picture of the succession of civilisations which have nurtured Tunisian soil.

Prestigious though it may be, the Bardo Museum is not the be-all and end-all of the history of Tunisia. The sites from which the various collections here have been taken should be the next step for the visitor anxious to further his knowledge of a Tunisia he has come to know and love.

MAP OF THE MAIN
ARCHAEOLOGICAL SITES

HIPPO-DIARRHYTUS
Bizerte

THABRACA
Tabarka

MATERA
Mateur

VTICA
Utica

KARTHAGO
Carthage

CLUPEA
Kélibia

VAGA
Béja

CINCARI
Testour

TUNES
Tunis

BVLLA REGIA
Bulla Régia

VTHINA
Oudna

THIGNICA
Aïn Tounga

NEAPOLIS
Nabeul

SIMITTHV
Chemtou

THVGGA
Dougga

THVBVRBO MAIVS
Hr. Kasbat

ZIQUA
Zaghouan

PVPPVT
Hammamet

MUSTI

SICCA-VENERIA
Le Kef

ALTHIBVROS
Médeina

MACTARIS
Maktar

HADRVMETVM
Sousse

VZITTA
Vzitta

Kairouan

A MMAEDARA
Haïdra

Mahdia

THYSDRVS
El Djem

SVFETVLA
Sbeitla

CILLIVM
Kasserine

ACHOLLA
Botria

THELEPTE
Feriana

TAPARVRA
Sfax

THAENAE
Thyna

CAPSA
Gafsa

MEDITERRANEAN SEA

TRITONIS LACVS
Chott El Jerrid

TACAPAE
Gabès

GIGTHIS
Bou Ghrara

GLOSSARY

Abbasides : Arab dynasty under the Baghdad caliphate (8th-16th centuries).
Aesculapius : the Roman god of medicine (Greek Asclepius).
Africa Romana : the Roman province more or less corresponding to today's Tunisia.
Aghlabides : Moslem dynasty, a vassal of the Abbasides. Their capital was Kairouan (9th-10th centuries).
Aphrodite : the Greek name of the goddess Venus
Apollo : the Greek god of the sun, arts and beauty
Apse : semi-circular part of a room
Astrolabe : an instrument of astronomy used to calculate latitudes.
Attica : the region around Athens in central Greece
Augustus : the first Roman emperor
Baal Hammon : the principal god in the Carthaginian pantheon. The Roman identified him with Saturn.
Baptistery : building in which Christian baptism is administered.
Bey (adj : **beylical**) : title given to the sovereign in Tunisia who was a vassal of the Sultan.
Calligraphy : the art of handwriting
Chemtou : a site in Tunisia famous for its marble quarries (generally yellow or pink).
Christogram : A Christian symbol made up of the first two letters of the Greek word *Christos*.
Cithara : a string musical instrument, Apollo's attribute.
Cyprian (Saint) : A latin writer and Father of the Church, bishop of Cartahge. Died as martyr in 258.
Demeter : the Greek goddess of agriculture (Roman Ceres)
Emblemata : a mosaic picture made of very fine tessarae and easily transportable.
Epitaph : an inscription on a tomb.
Fatimides : A Chi'ite dynasty that reigned over Egypt from the 10th to the 12th centuries.
Fibula : a brooch used to fasten articles of clothing
Fridigarium : the cold room in a Roman bath-house
Gens Augusta : members of the Emperor Augustus' family
Hafside : a dynasty from the Maghreb that reigned over Tunisia from 1228 to 1574.
Haouanet : a tomb carved in the rock.
Hellenistic : art and civilisation developed after the conquests of Alexander.
Hercules : hero of the Greco-Latin mythology, famous for his strength and many feats.
Hermes : the Greek messenger-god, protector of tradesmen and travellers (Roman Mercury).
Ifriqiya : name given by the Arab conquerors to the territory corresponding to Tunisia and Algeria today.
Koran : the Moslems' holy book
Krater : a type of wide-mouthed vessel used in Antiquity to hold a mixture of water and wine.

Kore : the daughter of Demeter, queen of the Underworld who rises up to the Earth in the early spring

Kufic : a type of Arabic decorative script

Libations : the pouring out of a liquid as an offering to a godhead

Libyc : the native population of central Tunisia before the arrival of the Romans.

Massinissa : king of the Numidians

Mausoleum : monumental tomb

Megalith (adj. **megalithic**) : prehistoric monument made of large rough stones.

Muizz Ibn Badis : a Zirid prince (cf infra)

Nave : part of a church reserved for the congregation

Nereid : sea nymph

Numidian : in Antiquity a native of what is today Algeria and Western Tunisia

Oecus : the reception room in a Roman house

Orant : in early Christian art a figure with hands upraised in prayer

Orpheus : a mythological figure whose music charmed wild beasts.

Paleochristian : early Christian art

Pantheon : all the gods of a mythology considered collectively.

Papyrus : kind of writing paper made from a plant growing on the banks of the Nile.

Pluto : another name for Hades, Greek god of the Underworld

Prophylactic : practice protecting from evil and diseases

Protohistory : period of history before the invention of writing

Protomeus : the forequarters of an animal projecting from a wall

Punic : relative to Carthaginian civilisation

Putto (pl. **putti**) : a naked child representing Cupid

Register : strip of decoration on different levels

Ribat : a fortress, the residence of soldier-monks

Sarcophagus : a stone coffin

Saturn : the principale god in North Africa, protector of sowing, identified with Baal Hammon.

Siggilated : red varnished ceramics of the Roman period

Stela : a stone sla raised as a tomb or commemorative monument.

Syncretism : the combination of various doctrines or religions

Tertullian : Latin writer born in Carthage (late 2nd-early 3rd centuries).

Thiase : the retinue of an ancient godhead.

Torah : parchment scrolls belonging to the Jewish religion bearing religious inscriptions, particularly the Law of Moses.

Tripod : three-legged seat from which the Pythia delivered the oracles of Apollo.

Triclinium : the dining-room in a Roman house

Trophy : an ornament made of a group of weapons or pieces of armour

Umeyades (or **Omeyades**) : a Moslem dynasty (6th-11th centuries)

Xenia : «still lives» in ancient paintings and mosaics.

Zirides : a Berber dynasty (973-1060).

* First occurence of words in the glossary is in italics in the text

GROUND FLOOR

I : Entrance hall, ticket office and shop
II : Prehistory
III/IV : Punic Department
V : Libyc Department
VI : Sarcophagus Corridor
VII : Thuburbo-Majus Corridor
VIII : Thuburbo-Majus Room
IX : Paleo-Christian Corridor
X : Paleo-Christian Room
XI : Bulla Regia Room
XII : Portraits of Emperors

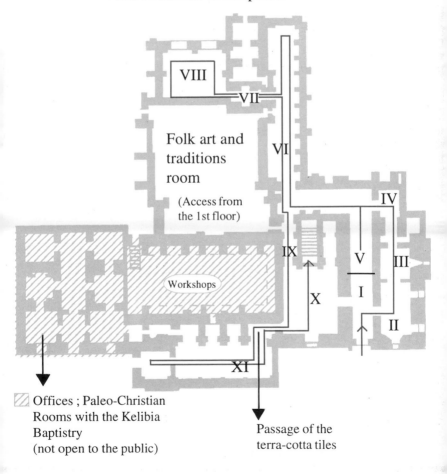

VIII

VII

Folk art and traditions room

(Access from the 1st floor)

VI

IV

IX

V

III

Workshops

X

I

II

XI

Offices ; Paleo-Christian Rooms with the Kelibia Baptistry (not open to the public)

Passage of the terra-cotta tiles

——————— Recommended direction of the visit

FIRST FLOOR

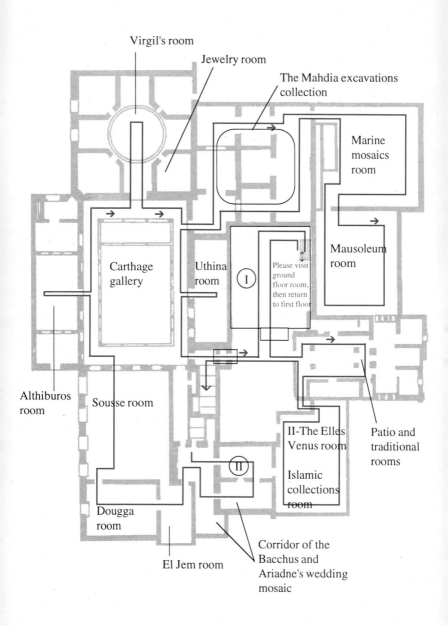

Virgil's room

Jewelry room

The Mahdia excavations collection

Marine mosaics room

Carthage gallery

Uthina room

I

Please visit ground floor room, then return to first floor

Mausoleum room

Althiburos room

Sousse room

II-The Elles Venus room

Islamic collections room

II

Patio and traditional rooms

Dougga room

El Jem room

Corridor of the Bacchus and Ariadne's wedding mosaic

———————————— Recommended direction of the visit

SECOND FLOOR

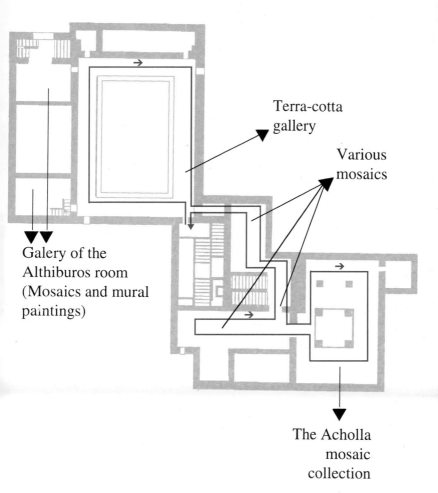

Terra-cotta gallery

Various mosaics

Galery of the Althiburos room (Mosaics and mural paintings)

The Acholla mosaic collection

———————— Recommended direction of the visit

Achevé d'imprimer sur les
presses des Imprimeries Réunies
Groupe Cérès Productions
6, Av. A. Azzam - 1002 Tunis
Juillet 1998